Yoga for Beginners:

Your Natural Way to Strengthen Your Body, Calming Your Mind and Be in The Moment

Susan Mori

Table of Contents

Introduction

I would like to thank you for purchasing the book _"Yoga for Beginners: Your Natural Way to Strengthen Your Body, Calming Your Mind, And Be in The Moment."_

One of the ancient forms of exercise that help to relax the body, mind and the soul is yoga. Yoga has been around for hundreds of years, and it is quite beneficial. You can improve your physical health as well as your overall mental and emotional wellbeing with Yoga.

Yoga isn't just about stretches and poses or asanas; it also includes several breathing exercises and meditation. If it is your first time considering yoga and you want a perfect book to help you get started, then look no further. In this book, you will learn everything you need to know about yoga. You will learn the basics of yoga, different yoga asanas, breathing exercises, meditation and useful tips to begin yoga. By the end of this book, it is quite likely that you will be eager to start your yoga routine as soon as possible.

Yoga is not rocket science, and you can learn it quickly, provided you follow the instructions in this book. If you are ready to learn about yoga, then let us start now!

Thank you once again for choosing this book, I hope you find it informative and helpful!

Chapter One: A Little about Yoga

The concept of Yoga originated in ancient India. Yoga means "union," and it is derived from the ancient Sanskrit word "yuj." It is a form of exercise that helps to balance the body, mind and spirit. There are many misconceptions about it, the most famous being that yoga is a religion. Yoga is clearly not a religion. In fact, it is a philosophy that dates back thousands of years.

Most people believe that yoga is the practice of particular poses known as asanas. Usually, people think of yoga as a physical exercise that consists of various twists, turns and stretches. Well, all this is only a part of yoga, but it is just the superficial layer of yoga. Yoga is a profound science that helps to align the body, mind and soul. Yoga isn't just a practice, but it is a way of life as well. The physical practice of yoga is so versatile that, regardless of how old, young, fit, or weak you are, you can perform these poses. The asanas range from simple to complex ones and, with practice, you can complete them all.

Believe it or not, but you may have been doing yoga, albeit unknowingly since you were a baby. Yoga places emphasis on specific movements we make unknowingly. However, Asanas are not the only forms of yoga that exist. In common parlance, the words yoga and asanas are used somewhat synonymously. Each different posture in yoga has a different physical benefit. The hectic lives that we lead today and the stress that we experience cause different physiological ailments. Yoga helps to release all the pent-up physical tensions and imbalances in our body. You can perform the yoga poses in quick succession, as it helps stimulates the body. All this, in turn, helps to improve your overall health.

What is the first thing that comes to your mind whenever someone says "yoga?" Perhaps you think of a lot of stretches and spandex! Yoga is so much more than stretches. If you ask ten people what they think about yoga, you will get ten different answers. It happens because the way one person experiences yoga is different from the way another person does. Your approach toward yoga will depend on your comfort level. No asana or technique will provide you any benefit if you aren't comfortable while you perform it.

Yoga is quite diverse, and it gives plenty of room for interpretation. Therefore, the way it is experienced differs from one person to another. You must not rush into trying advanced yoga poses. It is good to push your body, but you must also know when to stop.

Benefits of yoga

If you move and stretch your muscles, your flexibility will improve. You can feel a better range of motion even in the tight areas. After a while, you can experience flexibility in your hamstrings, back, shoulders and hips as well. With age, the flexibility of your muscles decreases, especially if you sit for a long time. This leads to pain as well as immobility. With the help of yoga, you can successfully reverse this process.

The yoga poses might seem deceptively simple. I mean, how difficult can it be to stretch your body? Well, don't be under any false impressions that yoga is just about stretching your body. Most yoga poses make use of your body weight in different ways. For instance, the tree pose, where you have to support your body weight on one leg or when you have to support your body weight with just your arms in the downward facing dog takes time, practice and considerable strength to hold these poses. You will be able to develop your muscle strength without even realizing that you are in fact doing so. ☐

Yoga doesn't help you to bulk up. However, it does help to build lean muscle and tone your body. Your muscle tone improves with yoga. It helps to shape all the lean and long muscles in your body like your legs, arms, back and abdomen. When you decide to lift weights to bulk up at the gym, you tend to lose flexibility. However, with yoga, you can develop six pack abs and maintain your muscle tone! If you want a toned body, then yoga is the best form of exercise.

Yoga requires balance. A significant benefit is the improvement of stability if you do yoga regularly. Not just that, it helps you to develop your core strength as well. ☐

Yoga requires you to perform movements that are of low intensity. It means that you can use your joints without doing them any damage. It strengthens the muscles around your joints and lessens the load on these muscles. If you have arthritis, then it's obvious you cannot perform any HIIT exercises. However, you can do yoga without any worry. It improves your mobility and strengthens your joints.

We all lead hectic lifestyles these days. Most of us tend to spend a lot of time hunched in front of our laptops. When you do this, you put a lot of pressure on your lower back. Therefore, it is no wonder that lower back problems are quite common. Even when you spend a lot of time driving, you will notice a sort of tightness all over your body. Your posture can lead to spinal compression and yoga counteracts all this. Certain yoga poses can reduce your lower back pain like the cobra pose.

We tend to take shallow breaths usually. In fact, most of us don't concentrate on how we breathe. Yoga has plenty of breathing exercises that will force you to focus on how you breathe. For instance, pranayama is all about conscious breathing. When you breathe properly, your body has an uninterrupted and a steady flow of oxygen. A better supply of oxygen will make you more active and it isn't just that. It helps to clear up your nasal passages and even calm your nervous system. You will learn about the different benefits of breathing exercises in the coming chapters.

The practice of yoga asanas is mostly physical. When you concentrate on what your body does, it tends to make your mind calmer. Meditation techniques are a significant part of yoga as well.

When you focus on the way you breathe, you won't obsess on your thoughts. All this can make you calmer as well. When your mind is calm, you can reorganize your thoughts. You can also disengage from thinking about anything negative. You cannot practice yoga when you are distracted. Intense concentration is a precondition to practicing yoga.

Any form of physical activity is helpful to relieve stress, even more so when you practice yoga. You have to concentrate, and therefore all your daily problems, big and small, seemingly melt away when you do yoga. While on the yoga mat, you won't be able to think about all the unnecessary troubles that weigh you down. It provides you with a clean break from the daily stress you experience. Yoga places great emphasis on the present moment and you won't have the time to think about past or future events. After a session of yoga, you will feel less stressed.

Yoga improves the connection between your body, mind and soul. It makes you aware of your body. Yoga helps you to learn to make subtle movements that help in better alignment of your body and mind. It helps you to form a bond with your physical and mental being. You also learn to accept your body without any judgment. When you can fully accept your body, you will feel more comfortable in your skin. All this helps to boost your self-confidence.

A rookie mistake that you must avoid is to perform yoga after a meal. You must never eat or drink anything before you practice yoga. Give your body a break of at least two hours before you decide to do yoga. The different breathing techniques and yoga asanas will make you nauseated if you try to do them on a full stomach. Always be careful of the way you align your body parts. If you aren't careful, you can hurt yourself. Start with simple asanas and increase the difficulty only after you master the basic asanas. If you experience any form of discomfort, stop doing yoga and consult a doctor at the earliest opportunity. Don't ignore any pain during your yoga experience, especially if you think that pain isn't reasonable.

You don't need any specific tools to perform yoga. Just a couple of simple things are necessary. You can practice yoga in the comfort of your home. Select a room that is spacious and calm. You will need a yoga belt, yoga mat, a yoga towel and a yoga block. Wear comfortable clothing and make sure that the material is absorbent. Wear tight or form-fitting clothes. It helps you to gauge whether your body is aligned or not. Always start the yoga practice with breathing exercises. You will learn about these in the coming chapters. Breathing exercises help to calm your mind and improve your focus. Also, before you hit the yoga mat, perform basic warm-up exercises as well.

Chapter Two: Yoga Breathing

We often tend to take shallow breaths, breathe in through the mouth and hardly use the diaphragm. We often use only a small portion of our lungs and our bodies don't get sufficient oxygen. With yoga breathing, you can breathe optimally. Here are the steps that you need to follow.

Step 1: Sit down on the floor or on the yoga mat. You can even lie down on the floor if you want to. Relax your body, get rid of all unnecessary thoughts and concentrate on your breathing.

Step 2: Inhale deeply through your nose. It allows you to take oxygen into your solar plexus. Now that you are conscious of your breathing, take in deep breaths. It helps to strengthen your body and improves the flow of oxygen to your brain. Push the air into your stomach, and you can feel your stomach expand. The oxygen reaches the lowest part of your lungs, then the diaphragm, before it comes out. When you inhale, your diaphragm needs to move downward. Keep your mouth shut and only inhale through your nose.

Step 3: Exhale through your nose. Follow the movement of your breath. It will move from your stomach to your diaphragm, your lungs and then to your nose. Relax your shoulders and don't tense up. When you breathe out, your diaphragm will move upwards, and it compresses your lungs to push the air out.

Step 4: There is a rhythm to yoga breathing. When you inhale, you have to hold your breath for the count of 7. Then retain your breath for a second before you exhale. Exhale to the count of 7, and then hold your breath for a second. So, the sequence is: Inhale - 7 seconds, retain for a second, exhale - 7 seconds and retain for a second.

Step 5: You can repeat this sequence a couple of times. You can also do this whenever you want to during the day. Whenever you feel stressed, you can perform this exercise to calm your mind. Always perform this exercise before you move on to any yoga poses.

Benefits of breathing exercises
The breathing exercise or Pranayama is a brilliant way to start your day. The best time to practice Pranayama is early in the morning. It is even better if you can practice pranayama outdoors. Nothing else can make you feel as good as fresh

air in the morning. If you want to do Pranayama in the morning, then do so on an empty stomach. In this section, you will learn about the different benefits of Pranayama.

1) Leads to detoxification

Did you know that your body tends to release about 70% of all the toxins in it through breathing? If you don't breathe efficiently, you stop your body from efficiently releasing all the pent-up toxins. It means that the pressure on all the other systems in the body will increase and it can cause illnesses as well. The natural waste of your body's metabolism is carbon dioxide. Your body releases carbon dioxide whenever you exhale.

2) Releases tension as well

How does your body feel when you are angry, tensed or scared? Does your body feel constricted? Does it feel like the muscles in your body are tensing up? Your muscles become tight and your breathing becomes quite shallow. Your body doesn't get the necessary oxygen when you are breathing in a shallow manner. So, deep breathing helps to cleanse the system and relax your muscles. Thereby, it helps to release tension as well. Not just that, it also helps to bring clarity to your emotions.

3) Relaxes mind and body

When your brain gets sufficient oxygen, it helps to reduce your anxiety levels. Pay attention to the way you breathe. Take in slow and deep breaths. When you inhale, concentrate on the action of inhalation and nothing else. Notice all those spots in your body that feel tight and wound up? Deep breathing helps to relax your body as well as your mind.

4) Massages your organs

Did you know that there is a connection between how you think, feel and your perspective toward life? For instance, how does your body react when it anticipates pain? Your body tenses up, and you hold your breath. If you practice deep breathing, you can reduce the pain that you experience. Don't let your body tense up. Your diaphragm moves during pranayama, and it helps to massage various internal organs like the stomach, liver, pancreas, small intestine and heart as well. It indirectly helps to improve the circulation of blood to these organs. Several breathing exercises can also help you to tone the abdominal muscles.

Correct breathing helps to increase the muscle in the body and strengthens the immune system. Hemoglobin is a pigment in blood that absorbs oxygen and transports it to all the cells in the body. When there is an increase in the supply of oxygen, it enriches your body. Breathing exercises help to improve your overall mood.

Getting ready for Pranayama

East or north is the best direction to do Pranayama. So, pick a spot that faces north or east. Place your yoga mat on the floor and sit cross-legged. Make sure that you stretch your spine and that your head, neck and chest are correctly aligned. You must not perform pranayama after you eat, bathe or engage in any sexual activity. There needs to be a gap of at least an hour. Pranayama is quite easy to perform. However certain people must not perform it. Pregnant women or those on their menstrual cycle must abstain from it. If you have any heart condition or recently had a cardiac arrest, then you must not perform pranayama. All those with low blood pressure should avoid it without the supervision of a teacher or a doctor. If you are ill or have fever, bronchitis or pneumonia, abstain from pranayama until you get better. Anyone who is undergoing chemo or radiation therapy is exempt from the list as well. It isn't recommended for anyone who has any psychological conditions either. If you have any pre-existing medical condition, it is better that you get a certificate of clearance from your doctor or physician if you want to do pranayama.

Before you move onto advanced pranayama techniques like Bhasktrika, you need to start with more straightforward exercises like Nadi shodhona. Nadi shodhona helps to purify the nervous system. The best method to start with is alternate nostril breathing.

Alternate nostril breathing

The Sanskrit name of the alternate nostril breathing technique is Anuloma Viloma. As the name suggests, this pranayama exercise requires you to breathe through the alternate nostrils of your nose. You will primarily be breathing only through one nostril at a time. It is a part of Nadi Shodhona or the purification of the nervous system. To perform this exercise, find a comfortable spot for yourself. You can either sit on the floor or on a chair with your feet firmly placed on the floor. Take deep breaths with your left nostril. Do this ten times and then shift to the other nostril. It doesn't take more than 5 minutes to perform this calming exercise.

When you perform Anuloma Villoma, keep one of your nostrils closed at all times. You have to make use of your right-hand thumb, ringer finger and little finger to close your nostril. To close your right nostril, use your thumb. To close your left nostril, use your ring and little fingers. Keep your mouth shut and don't inhale or exhale through your mouth. Don't make any sounds while you inhale or exhale. □

There are two rounds to practice this technique. In the first round, start by focusing on your breath for a minute. Observe how air flows from both your nostrils. Raise your right hand and form the pranayama mudra.

Lift your right hand so that your thumb, little finger and ring finger are pointing outward. The other two fingers need to be bent inward. To close your right nostril, place your thumb gently on it and inhale through the left nostril. Once you inhale, you have to close the left nostril with your ring and little finger. Only after you close your left nostril can you exhale through the right one. After you exhale through the right nostril, inhale through the same one. To exhale, you have to close the right nostril and let go of your breath through the left one. To simplify it all, in the first round, you have to perform the following four steps.

1. *Inhale through the left nostril*
2. *Exhale from the right nostril*
3. *Inhale from the right nostril, and*
4. *Then exhale from the left nostril.*

After ten rounds, place your hands on your knees and concentrate on your breathing for a minute. For round two, you have to position your left hand in the pranayama mudra. Repeat the steps mentioned above, but with the other nostril.

So, you will inhale through your right nostril, exhale through the left one, then inhale through the same nostril, and finally exhale through the right nostril. After you perform ten rounds, place your hands on your knees and focus on your breathing for a minute. It is as simple as that.

There are various benefits to this exercise. You will feel at peace and relaxed. It is believed that this form of pranayama helps to clear 72,000 channels or nadis in the human body. If you want to purify your respiratory system, then this is the best breathing exercise. It helps to reduce stress and anxiety and offers all the other benefits that were discussed earlier.

Chapter Three: Yoga Poses

If you are new to yoga, there are a couple of postures that you need to learn so that you can feel more comfortable. There are more than 300 poses in yoga. In this chapter, you will learn about the basic yoga poses for a beginner. You can use these poses to create your yoga practice. You can lengthen and deepen the practice of any yoga pose according to your comfort level.

The Mountain Pose

The Sanskrit name of this pose is Tadasana.

Steps: Stand on the yoga mat. Press down on your toes and keep your feet together. You will engage your quadriceps in this pose. You can feel the stretch in your kneecaps and thighs. Pull in your abdominal muscles as you stretch your body upward. Stretch yourself as much as you can. Your palms must face inwards, and you can feel your shoulder blades open up and come towards each other. Imagine that a string is pulling your body upward. Breathe in deeply through your nose and hold your breath for the count of 5-8 seconds before you exhale through your nose.

If you want to challenge yourself, then try to balance without any support. It is an essential standing yoga pose.

The Chair Pose

Utkatasana is the Sanskrit name of The Chair Pose.

Steps: Start with the mountain pose. Lift your arms up and reach up with your hands. The pose mimics your posture when you sit in a chair with your back straight. Shift your weight and elongate your upper torso as much as possible. You can improve your comfort level in this pose. Then you must bend your bones towards your heels. Rest your hands on the top of your thighs. Place the base of your palms in the crease of your groin and push your thighs toward your heels. Dig your heels into the yoga mat to improve your balance. While you do this, lift your sitting bones toward your pelvis.

As the name suggests, you have to mimic the pose of sitting in a chair, sans the chair. It isn't difficult! You use your thigh muscles to hold the pose. While you do this, you have to keep your arms pointing upward near your ears. Keep your legs squeezed together, for better balance. Hold this position for fifteen seconds. You can even modify it and hold it for longer, but that depends on your strength and endurance. Repeat this exercise three times, and you can work your way toward ten reps. It not only strengthens the muscles in your legs but also facilitates the movement of your sexual energy to your energy centers.

The Downward-facing Dog Pose

The Sanskrit name of this pose is Adho Mukha Svanasana.

Steps: Place yourself on the yoga mat on all fours. Your wrists must be in perfect alignment with your shoulders and your knees with your hips. Tuck in your toes and lip your hips off the floor with your arms and pull them towards your heels. You can slightly bend your knees if your hamstrings are too tight. Push your hips backward and straighten your legs. You can stretch your body more by pushing your hands outwards. Rest your body weight on your palms and move your elbows towards each other. Hollow out your abdomen and engage your legs. Hold this pose for 5-8 seconds and then drop back onto your hands and knees.

To increase the stretch in the back of your legs, lift yourself up on the balls of your feet. Pull your heels up by about half an inch away from the floor. Lengthen your form by pulling up from the heels of your foot.

Head to Knee Bend

The Sanskrit name of this pose is Janu Sirsasana

Steps: Sit on the yoga mat and stretch your legs in front of you. Then inhale deeply through your nose. Bend your right knee inwards, towards your body. Exhale through your nose. Now bend forward so that your head lies somewhere close to your knee. With practice, your body becomes quite flexible. Hold this pose for 5 seconds.

Hands to Heart Pose

The Sanskrit name of this pose is Anjali Mudra

Steps: Stand on the yoga mat with your feet together. Keep your back and shoulders straight. Bring your hands towards your heart, as you would while praying. Join your hands in the prayer pose. Don't breathe with your mouth. Inhale and exhale through your nose.

Wind-relieving Pose
The Sanskrit name of this pose is
Pavanamuktasana

Steps: Lie down on your back on the yoga mat.
Extend your arms and legs. Inhale deeply
through your nose. Draw one of your knees
towards your chest and use your hands for
support. Once you do this, exhale deeply through
your nose. Hold this pose for ten seconds.

The Hero Pose

The Sanskrit name for this pose is Virasana.

Steps: Kneel down on the yoga mat. Straighten your back and let your buttocks come to rest on the heels of your foot while your toes touch the mat. Now, slowly place your hands behind your back and try to reach the backs of your feet. Inhale and exhale deeply through your nose while you perform this pose.

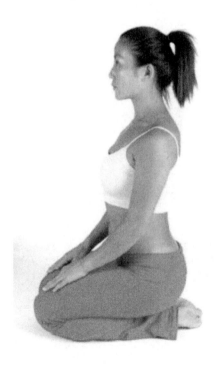

The Standing Forward Bend

The Sanskrit name of this pose is Uttanasana.

Steps: Stand on the yoga mat and keep your back straight. Gently bend downwards and try to reach for your toes. You can even use the yoga belt for additional support. You can secure your balance by holding onto the back of your ankles. Stay in this position while you breathe in and out deeply through your nose.

The Infinity Pose
The Sanskrit name of this pose is Ananthasana

Steps: Lie on the yoga mat on your right side. Support your head with your right hand. Now slowly raise your right leg over your head. You can grab the back of your hamstrings for better support. Lift your knees and hold this position for 15 seconds. Don't let go of your leg abruptly, and slowly ease out of this pose.

The Knee to Chest Pose

The Sanskrit name of this pose is Pavanamuktasana.

Steps: Lie down on the yoga mat on your back. Gradually draw your left knee inwards and towards your chest. While you do this, breathe in deeply through your nose. To secure yourself in this pose, you can place your hand below the left kneecap. Once your knee touches your chest, exhale deeply through your nose. Hold this pose for ten seconds before you ease up.

The Scale Pose

The Sanskrit name for this pose is Tolasana.

Steps: You have to sit cross-legged on the yoga mat. Now, place your palms on the floor so that they are next to your hips. Push hard against your hands on the floor and exhale through your nose. Contract your abdominal muscles. Gently lift your buttocks from the floor and your legs away from the floor. Hold this position to the count of 15. Slowly, lower your buttocks and your legs toward the floor again. Stay like this for 5 seconds and then relax your body.

The Bridge Pose

The Sanskrit name of this pose is Setu Bandha Naukasana.

Steps: Lie down on your back on the yoga mat. Gently bend your knees so that your feet are planted firmly on the ground. You can use your yoga belt for additional support. Gently raise your off the floor and place your hands underneath. Inhale and exhale deeply through your nose while you do this.

The Bow Pose

The Sanskrit name of this pose is Urdva Chakrasana.

Steps: Lie down on your belly on the yoga mat. Place your hands next to your chest. Inhale and exhale deeply through your nose. Now, slowly raise your legs and try to reach your legs with your hands. You can use a yoga belt for extra support. While you lift yourself, deeply inhale and exhale through your nose.

The Cat Pose

The Sanskrit name of this pose is Marjaryasana.

Steps: Kneel down on the yoga mat and support your body weight with your hands. Face downwards and arch your back so that your feet, knees and hands are placed firmly on the ground. Inhale and exhale deeply through your nose. The pose you assume must be that of a cat when it crouches. Hold this position for ten seconds before you relax.

The Prone Cobra Pose

The Sanskrit name of this pose is Prone Bhujangasana.

Lie down on your belly on the yoga mat. Your hands need to rest on your body. Inhale and exhale deeply through your nose and hold this pose for 10 seconds. This pose helps to calm your mind, correct your posture and helps with any ankle or knee injuries.

The Puppy Dog on Chair Pose

The Sanskrit name of this pose is Uttana Shishosana (in the original version of this pose).

Steps: Stand on the yoga mat with your feet slightly apart. This pose helps to strengthen your abdominal muscles. Now raise your hands over your head and join them together. Gently bend your torso forward. Stay in this pose for ten seconds. Inhale and exhale deeply through your nose while you perform this asana.

The Elevated Peacock Pose

The Sanskrit name of this pose is Mayurasana Pincha. It is an intermediate/advanced yoga pose.

Steps: Place your yoga mat against a wall for support. You have to kneel down on the yoga mat. Place your hands forward on the mat and firmly place your palms on the mat. Now, raise your upper body toward your hands. Try to lift your legs up while you do this. The idea of this pose is to perform a headstand. You have to support your entire torso on your palms and head. That's why you need to lean against a wall for some support. It isn't a comfortable pose, and you might not raise yourself off the ground initially. You can ask someone to hold your legs up for better balance. Breathe in and out deeply when you do this. This asana helps to improve your upper body strength and strengthens your abdominal muscles too.

The Warrior Pose 1

The Sanskrit name of this pose is Virabhadrasana.

Steps: You have to stand straight on the yoga mat. Now, place your left leg sideward. Lower yourself onto your right knee (almost like a lunge) and stretch your left leg outward. Stretch your body as much as you can. Slowly raise your arms above your head, and your palms need to face one another. Your hands must be raised above your head, and your hands must be clasped in the traditional prayer pose. Inhale and exhale deeply through your nose.

The Cobra Pose

The Sanskrit name of this pose is Bhujangasana.

Steps: You have to lie down on the yoga mat on your belly. Make sure that you spread your legs when you lie down. Let your forehead rest on the ground and keep your shoulders relaxed. Bend your elbows and place your forearms on the mat like you would when you do a push-up. Now, elevate your upper torso slowly while your hands rest on the floor near your hips. Elongate your upper body as much as you can. You should feel a stretch in your lower-back muscles. The pose you assume should resemble that of a cobra when it is ready to strike. Inhale deeply when you raise your hips and exhale deeply when you lower your hips. Breathe only through your nose. The cobra pose is not just good for your sexual health, but it helps with any lower back pain that you experience. It also helps to correct your posture. Place yourself on all fours, and your arms should be shoulder width apart, while your knees are almost touching. You have to slowly lower your body while you keep your upper torso elevated. Keep your arms straight, and your elbows should point toward your body. You can look upwards, provided you don't have any neck issues. You can rest on your forearms if you feel any discomfort in your lower back or abdomen. The basic idea is to imitate the pose of a cobra when it is ready to strike. Initially, hold this pose for 30 seconds, and you can increase it slowly to three minutes. It stimulates your sexual centers of energy to enhance your performance and vitality.

Butterfly Pose

Place your mat on the floor. Sit down on the mat and make sure that your back is straight. Now, bend your knees so that the soles of your feet are pressed together. Place them as close to your crotch as you can. Initially, your knees might not touch the floor, and that's okay. Hold the butterfly pose and focus on your inner thighs. Push down on your knees so that they are as close to the floor as they possibly can be. You will feel slight tension in your thigh muscles when you perform this pose. Relax, it happens and it is natural. You can close your eyes to improve your focus.

Hold this pose for three minutes. It helps to tone the channels of sexual energy and also your reproductive organs.

Seated forward bend

Place the mat on the floor. Sit down on the mat and keep your back straight. Stretch your legs in front of you. Now lean forward and move your arms towards your toes. Let your knees stretch ahead and don't lock them. Allow your upper torso to relax and feel the slight stretch in your back and the back of your legs. However, don't overstretch your body, or you will hurt yourself. Take long and deep breaths through your nostrils. If you are flexible, then you can even grab your shins, ankles or toes (if you are incredibly limber). Hold this pose for a minute. Then slowly return to your original position. Repeat this pose three times in a session. If you want to increase your mobility, then this is a good pose, and it also helps to stimulate the sexual energy in your body.

Runner's Stretch

The runner's stretch is just a fancy name for a lunge. You have to stand straight on the yoga mat, and then place your right leg forward a few feet. When you do this, bend your right knee and keep your left leg stretched out straight. Do not allow your knee to go past your ankle when you stretch. You can either place your hands on your hips or put them on either side of your right foot for better support. You will feel the muscles in your left leg stretch, and it strengthens your right leg. Hold this pose to the count of ten deep and slow breaths. Once you do this, return to the standing posture on your mat. Now, repeat the same with your other leg. This position helps to strengthen your pelvic floor muscles, improves your flexibility as well as stamina.

Sat kriya pose

Sit on the heels of your feet or your feet and keep your knees bent. If you feel that's difficult, kneel down. You can even place a towel under your knees for additional padding. Now, slowly stretch your arms above your head. Your elbows should be close to your head. If that's not comfortable for you, merely stretch your arms upward as high as possible. Interlock all your fingers except your index fingers. Your index fingers should point straight up. Cross one thumb over the other. Close your eyes and start the following set of contractions. If you want to, you can say "sat" whenever you inhale and "kriya" when you exhale. You have to inhale and exhale through your nose and close your mouth. You will notice that your abdominal muscles will contract and it all starts from your navel. Inhale through your nose and contract the muscles around your stomach. You will feel slight contractions in the muscles around your navel, rectum and your groin. It is known as the "root" lock. Hold your breath in for a moment, visualize the movement of energy from your buttocks, along the length of your spine to your head. Exhale through your nose slowly, release the root lock and then do it twice. Rest for a couple of seconds and repeat the exercise. You should do this exercise for at least three minutes, and you can slowly work your way toward ten minutes. If your limbs feel tired, take a break for a couple of seconds. However, try to do this for at least three minutes. It is a beneficial pose to tone your sexual organs, and it helps with any sexual dysfunction as well.

Frog Pose

To start this pose, you have to squat on your toes. Place your feet apart while your heels are pressed together. Lift your arms to gain better balance. Breathe in through your nose and stand up while you lower your head towards your knees. Lower your heels as you stand up straight. Make sure that your fingers touch the floor. It is okay if you aren't able to straighten your legs fully. Now, slowly exhale through your nose. You have completed one rep of this exercise. Inhale as you start the next rep while you return to the squatting position. You can gradually work your way up to ten reps of the frog pose. Of course, you can do more reps if your body permits. It might sound deceptively simple, but it does take a lot of effort. Don't hold your breath in and breathe slowly.

It is an excellent pose to improve your sexual health, tone the muscles in your legs and speed up your heart rate. If you have any issues with your knees, you should skip this exercise. If you don't have any knee trouble, then please go ahead. However, stop whenever your knees hurt. You can suffer from hemorrhoids if you do too many reps of the frog pose. Also, take a break whenever you feel dizzy or lightheaded.

Plough Pose

Lie down on the yoga mat. Now, draw your knees towards your chest. Roll backward and let your legs extend way past your head. Stretch your legs as much as you can. You can support your back with your hands. In this pose, your toes should touch the ground. Well, it will take you a while to get there. If you are quite limber, then you can do this pose easily. You should feel the muscles in your legs stretch and some contraction in your abdomen. Don't overdo it or else you can seriously hurt your back. Take in long and deep breaths. Hold this pose for anywhere between 1 to 3 minutes. If you feel dizzy or lightheaded, stop immediately.

It is an ideal position to enhance your sexual system. However, for a beginner, it is a good idea to take it slow. Make sure that you don't put any unnecessary strain on the muscles in your back, neck and hamstrings.

Rock pose

It is a relaxing and straightforward pose for your body. Place yourself on the edge of your yoga mat and tuck yourself into a ball. Your knees should be bent towards your chest and wrap your arms around your shins. You mainly have to curl up into a ball. Breathe like you usually do and rock onto your back. Once you rock onto your back, roll back again to a seated pose. Don't roll onto your neck, or you can hurt yourself seriously. Continue to roll like a ball for thirty seconds and work your way towards a minute.

This pose helps to strengthen your core and stimulate the centers of sexual energy in your body.

The Bridge Pose

Lie down on the yoga mat and place your feet as close to your butt as you possibly can while your knees are bent. Gently lift your torso upwards while you press down with your feet. Tighten the muscles in your thighs and buttocks. Lift your navel off the ground as high as you can. Hold the bridge for at least thirty seconds and slowly work your way towards three minutes. It is a commanding position. When you complete a set, gradually lower your back onto the yoga mat, one vertebra at a time. Lower yourself until you are lying on the mat with your knees bent. Repeat this exercise three times. It helps to strengthen your pelvic muscles, and it also enhances your core and legs. You can feel the sexual energy move through your body from the base of your spine to your head.

Corpse Pose

Well, the corpse pose is the easiest yoga asana there is. As the name suggests, you only have to lie down on your yoga mat like a corpse. Close your eyes and place your hands on either side of your body. Breathe regularly and don't let any worries distract you. Inhale and exhale through your nose. The Shavasana or the corpse pose is the best way to end your yoga session. If you like listening to music, then play some soothing music. You can do this for up to 11 minutes.

If you want to improve your sexual health, then these positions will undoubtedly come in handy.

Chapter Four: Yoga Meditation

Yoga is a Sanskrit word that means union with the cosmos or divine energy. It involves various stretching exercises, and it has been around for thousands of years. Well, by now you know the history of yoga and the multiple benefits it offers.

If you want to practice yoga meditation, there are three steps that you have to follow. The first step is to create an environment that's conducive to meditation. The second step is to perform the basic poses. The third step is to focus on your mind, body, and soul. □

Create a meditation spot

The first step is to create a quiet environment. Select a place that is free of clutter and loud noises. You should feel comfortable if you want to practice yoga or meditation. If the spot is too noisy, then you cannot concentrate, especially if you are a beginner. An ideal location should be devoid of all electronic gadgets. Or find a place where you can block all the external sounds. It will be helpful if you can find a room where natural light filters in through the windows. If not, the lighting should be soft and not too harsh. Flickering lights are a distraction, aren't they? Select a room with some natural heat, light and air. It is not just the sounds that are a distraction. Even machinery can be quite uncomfortable to listen to. If you cannot do yoga or meditate in the open, find a place that has some radiant heat. Create cross ventilation by opening a door or a window. Let some fresh air into the room. If your tummy is full, you will relax too much, and it will make you drowsy. At the same time, if your yoga or meditation session is too close to meal time, your hunger pangs can be quite distracting. Perhaps you can practice meditation a couple of hours before your mealtime or a couple of hours after your meal. If not, you can always have a light snack before you meditate. It is essential to provide your body with the necessary sustenance to keep it functioning. Before you meditate or perform yoga, do some light stretching or warm-up exercises. Warm up exercises will get the blood pumping in your body and will make you feel relaxed. Not just that, your concentration will also improve while you meditate. If your body feels limber, then you can sit for longer. Concentrate on your back and your core for a couple of minutes. Simple twists and bends will do the trick. You can practice Sukshma yoga before you meditate. To do Sukshma yoga, you have to gently squeeze your eyebrows a couple of times using your fingers. Roll your eyes a couple of times. Then rub your jawline as well as your temples to relax your facial muscles. Grab your ears and slowly tug them downwards. □

Perform meditative poses

For starters, sit upright. You can rest on any surface you want, as long as it allows you to sit correctly. You can sit on the floor or a chair. Don't make your body rigid and let it feel limber. Sitting cross-legged while you meditate is quite common. However, that's not the only way to relax. You can alternate the leg that rests on top while you meditate. Being comfortable is the main point. For better spinal alignment, you can gently tug on your chin.

Once you find a comfortable spot for yourself and have settled in, the next step is to follow the techniques of deep breathing. Focus on your breath and nothing else. You can count the number of times you inhale and exhale through your nose. Or you can even perform Nadi shodan. Nadi shodan is a technique of pranayama. Lift your right hand so that your thumb, little finger and ring finger are pointing outward while the rest curl inward. To close your right nostril, place your thumb gently on it and inhale through the left nostril. Once you inhale, you have to close the left nostril with your ring and little finger. Only after you close your left nostril can you exhale through the right one. After you exhale through the right nostril, inhale through the same one. To exhale, you have to close the right nostril and let go of your breath through the left one. Once you do this with your right nostril, repeat the same steps with your left nostril.

Another breathing exercise that you can practice before meditating is to perform Samasthiti. The pose of Samasthiti is quite similar to the posture of an army person standing to attention. You have to be mindful of your balance and steadiness. Once you stand to attention, join your palms together (like you would when you pray). Breathe in slowly and raise your hands over your head. When you exhale, return your hands to your chest. Do this exercise for two minutes to calm your mind.

The next exercise that you can do is to perform the cow pose. Get on all fours and place your palms under your shoulders to support yourself. Breathe in deeply and raise your head along with your upper torso. While you elevate your upper body, lower your spine slowly towards the floor. You are mostly pushing your spine closer to your stomach. Complete this position by returning to a perfectly aligned back while you exhale.

The next asana you can perform to meditate is Vajrasana. To perform Vajrasana, you have to assume a sitting position. Once you do that, place your hands to the side and move your left foot so that it is in contact with your left buttock. Repeat the same with your right foot. Once you do this, you will be in a squatting position. You can lean forward and shift your body weight onto your knees. Lean backward onto the space available between your heels. Breathe like you usually do for a couple of minutes. At the end of this pose, your toes should be touching one another. Make sure that you keep your core coiled to encourage better posture. Your body should be upright while you perform this pose.

The last meditative yoga exercise you can perform is ujjayi breathing. Ujjayi breath is a long and smooth breath. It will not only calm you down but will make you feel quite energetic as well. You have to sit cross-legged on the floor. Try to relax your body and mind. Imagine that you are taking in deep and slow breaths (like breathing through a straw). Now exhale slowly (through the same imaginary straw). Make your breathing as slow and deliberate as you possibly can.

Focus on your body, mind, and soul
Forget about all the distractions. Don't think about any of your daily stresses and worries. The

first step of meditation yoga is to embrace all the different things that go on in your life. Acknowledge all the chaos that you feel. You cannot only ignore your worries. Instead, embrace them and accept them all. After all, you are just a human being and concerns are a significant part of human nature. Only when you recognize all the distractions, can you move beyond them and focus on yourself. Instead, concentrate on your body. Focus your attention inwards, towards the base of your spine. Focus your attention on the center of your body, to your spinal column and all the different parts of your body. Take stock of all the different parts of your body and all your different senses. Acknowledge all that you feel and think. Think about how your body functions and how each of the various parts functions like a well-oiled machine. Notice if you feel any pain or discomfort. If you want to reach a higher level of concentration while you meditate, you should will your mind to become silent. You have to set your mind at ease, and you can do so by concentrating on your breathing. If you want to become aware of your mind, then you should follow the four functions of the mind. The four functions of the mind are to observe, accept, understand and train. You have to see all the impressions present in your mind like ego, judgments or any prejudices. The next step is to accept all the observations you have without being critical of them. Forget about whether a particular observation is good or bad, and don't berate yourself for it. The next step is to understand your thought process - the way your mind functions and discerns things. The final step is to train your mind. You need to realize that you are in complete control of your mind and it isn't the other way around. You should train your consciousness.

Once you do this, the next step is to focus on a single object. If you have just started to try meditation, during the initial phases, it might be difficult for you to concentrate fully. It is quite likely that your attention will lapse. Whenever you feel like your attention sways, you should redirect it towards a specific object. Try to focus on a single item - like a piece of floorboard, a spot on the wall or even a stationary object. At the end of your meditation session, you should bring your mind to attention. Take charge of your mind and be aware of all the small changes in your body. You can lightly ball your fists for a couple of minutes. Alternatively, you can even flex the muscles in your calf. A simple way to focus on your muscles is by smiling.

Chapter Five: Surya Namaskars

One of the most useful yoga practices is that of Surya Namaskar. The literal translation of the phrase Surya Namaskar is sun salutation. The Sanskrit word Surya implies sun and Namaskar mean salutation. It helps to cleanse your body, mind and soul. The best time to do Surya Namaskars is at daybreak on an empty stomach. If you aren't a morning person, you can perform this routine whenever you want to. However, make sure that you perform it on an empty stomach. If not, give your body at least two hours after your meal before you practice Surya Namaskars. This exercise routinely engages all the essential muscle groups in your body. It is advisable to do 108 sets in a day. It might not be possible to do all this in the first attempt. You can start with 20 and slowly increase the number. You can even do Surya Namaskars in sets.

Step 1. Pranamasana

Pranam means to pray in Sanskrit and Pranamasana is a prayer pose. Place the yoga mat on the floor and stand on the edge of your mat. Place your legs close together and let your arms rest by your side. Inhale deeply through your nose while you lift your arms above your head. Exhale slowly through your nose and bring your palms together (like you would while you pray). Place your joined hands in front of your chest.

Step 2. Hasta Uttanasana

This pose is also known as The Raised Arms Pose. This asana requires you to inhale deeply through your nose and lift your arms over your head. Then move your arms backward slowly. While you do this, your biceps should be close to your ears. The goal is to stretch your body, but backward. Push your upper torso as much as you can.

Step 3. Hastapaadasana

From the previous pose, you have to transition into Hastapaadasana. This pose is also known as The Hand to Foot Pose. Exhale deeply through your nose, slowly raise your body upwards and then bend your body forward. While you do this, your palms should face downward, and your fingertips should align with your toes. If you feel any discomfort, you can slightly bend your knees. It is just a simple forward bend. With time and practice, it gets easier, and you don't have to bend your knees. Exhale deeply through your nose and move your hands towards the floor. The goal is to touch your toes or your feet with your hands. The literal meaning of this pose is to make your hands meet your feet. It makes your body limber and strengthens your back.

Step 4. Ashwa Sanchalanasana

From the previous pose, you have to transition into Ashwa Sanchalanasana. This pose is also known as The Equestrian Pose. You have to inhale deeply through your nose and gradually push your left leg backward. Stretch your left leg as much as you can. Bring your right foot forward and plant your right foot firmly on the mat. Place your hands so that the right foot is in between your hands.

Step 5. Kumbhakasana

This pose is also known as the Plank Pose, and you transition into it after the previous pose. Don't exhale immediately after the last step and hold your breath. In the meanwhile, you have to slowly stretch your left leg backward to join your right leg. Balance your body weight with the help of your toes and hands. Your body should be perfectly aligned. You have to perform a simple plank and hold the pose for 5 seconds.

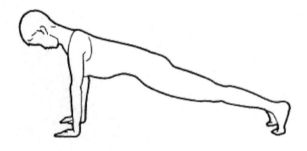

Step 6. Ashtanga Namaskara

The literal translation of this pose means, "Salute with Eight Parts." Gently move your knees towards the floor while you maintain the plank pose. Exhale through your nose while you do this. Slightly bend your knees towards the ground, and your kneecaps should touch the mat. Lower your chin and your chest so that they reach the mat too. Altogether, eight parts of your body will touch the floor and these parts are your chin, chest, hands, knees and feet.

Step 7. Bhujangasana

This pose is also known as the Cobra Pose. From the previous posture, you have to transition into this pose. Your arms should be shoulder width apart, and your knees should be close together. Slowly lower your body while your upper torso stays elevated. Keep your arms straight, and your elbows should point inwards and towards your body. You can look upwards if you don't have any neck issues. Balance your body weight on your hands. So, make sure that your palms are firmly planted on the mat.

Step 8. Adho Mukha Svanasana

This pose is known as the Downward Facing Dog Pose. You have to transition to this pose from Bhujangasana. Exhale deeply through your nose after the previous step and curl your toes. Slowly raise your hips off the ground. Pivot your hips so that your body forms the shape of an inverted V. Now, push on your heels while you keep your head down. Arch your shoulders as much as you can. After this step, you will repeat the first four steps in the reverse order.

Step 9. Ashwa Sanchalanasana

Inhale deeply through your nose and gradually push your left leg backward. Stretch your left leg as far as you can. Bring your right foot forward and plant your right foot firmly on the mat. Place your hands such that the right foot is in between your hands. You will support most of your bodyweight with your arms.

Step 10. Hastapaadasana

Exhale deeply through your nose, slowly raise your body upwards and then bend your body forward. While you do this, your palms should face downward and your fingertips should align with your toes. It is a simple forward bend. Exhale deeply through your nose and move your hands towards the floor. The goal is to touch your toes or your feet with your hands.

Step 11. Hasta Uttanasana

Inhale deeply through your nose and lift your arms above your head. Then you have to move your arms backward slowly. While you do this, your biceps should be close to your ears. The goal is to stretch your body, but backward. Push your upper torso as much as you can.

Step 12. *Pranamasana*
End the exercise with the prayer pose.

Now that you are familiar with all the twelve steps of Surya Namaskar, the next step is to practice it.

Chapter Six: Tips before You Start Yoga

If you are new to yoga, you will have queries about what you are getting into, the yoga gear and equipment you will need and how you must prepare yourself for yoga. If you know what to expect and what will work ahead of time, you will undoubtedly feel more comfortable.

Yoga is often done barefoot. So, you don't need any special shoes for yoga. If you want, you can wear socks. However, it is better to do yoga barefoot. It provides better grip. You don't need any specific pants for yoga. As long as the pants you wear allow you to move freely and don't restrict your limbs, it is good. Yoga pants, leggings or even sweatpants will suffice. You don't have to go shopping specifically for yoga gear. Make sure that the clothes you wear are not too short or too loose. It is quite annoying if you have to keep pulling your pants up after every stretch. Always avoid pants that don't stretch like formal trousers or jeans. Anything that you can wear to the gym, you can wear for yoga too. A well-fitted top is the best fit for yoga. A t-shirt that is baggy or loose will slide down whenever you bend over. Sleeveless tops and well-fitted tops are ideal. Yoga includes a lot of poses where you need to stretch your body and bend quite a bit. So, the clothes you wear must not ride up every time you bend over.

Make sure that you have a yoga mat, a water bottle and a towel with you. A yoga mat is essential, and you need one before you start doing yoga. It is a good idea to invest in a yoga mat. The yoga mat you opt for must provide you a good grip, and it needs to be soft. Almost all yoga poses need a yoga mat. A water bottle always comes in handy. Keep a bottle of water nearby when you start doing yoga. If you tend to sweat a lot, then yoga will make you sweat more. So, you need a hand towel to wipe your sweat away. There are some yoga props that you can invest in as well. However, as a beginner, you don't necessarily need these props initially.

Never have a heavy meal before you do yoga. Once you move, everything starts to churn in your stomach, and you might feel sick if your stomach is full. So, make sure that you give your body at least an hour before you do yoga. You can always have a light snack before yoga, but it is better to avoid it. Before you start doing yoga, you need to do a few warm-up exercises. As with any other form of exercise, warming up will make your body limber and remove any stress from your muscles. You can do a few basic stretches or even sit cross-legged on the mat and meditate.

Alignment is an important aspect of yoga poses. You need to concentrate on the alignment of your body if you want to avoid hurting yourself. Start out slow, and you can make your way up to more complex yoga poses.

Chapter Seven: Tips for Beginner's

Yoga is an excellent form of exercise. Irrespective of whether you are a beginner at yoga, or are a yoga veteran, the pleasure that comes from yoga remains the same. In fact, it is quite likely that the experience of a beginner will be more joyous than that of an experienced practitioner. Since you are just starting to do yoga, you might run into a few pesky problems during yoga practice. For instance, the vocabulary used in yoga will probably seem a little awkward until you get the hang of it. For most Westerners, Sanskrit sounds very exotic, and western eyes might glaze over rather swiftly. If someone asks you to read something like "pashchimottanasana," you might fumble a little. Another problem that you can run into is with the execution of the yoga poses or asanas. Don't worry! Even if a specific asana sounds strange, it is designed for a precise reason. Thoughts like "Do I have to sit like that?" "That pose certainly doesn't look comfortable?" "Can I even stretch my body like that?" or "I am no gymnast to perform these asanas" might pop into your head. Well, with a little practice, you will be able to perform even the most complicated asanas - maybe not immediately, but eventually, you will! All beginners need a little empathy along the way. After all, you are just getting started.

The most challenging aspect of yoga as a beginner is to create a yoga routine at home. To build a yoga routine for yourself, you need to make a list of techniques and poses and then create a yoga routine for yourself. Another question that will frequently come to your mind is "Is this pose important? Can't I skip it?" Well, whenever such a question pops into your head, you must not pay any heed to such doubts. Each pose has a specific purpose and a particular effect on your body. In this section, you will learn some tips that will come in handy for a beginner. Most of these tips are practical, simple and will provide the necessary encouragement to keep you going. However, all these tips have a common denominator - they all call for action. It certainly doesn't make any sense to arm yourself with all the knowledge if you don't put it to use. So, go through the points listed in this chapter carefully, and incorporate these tips into your daily routine. Well, if you are ready, let us get started without further delay:

Tip #1 - Maintain a yoga journal

After a yoga session, you will have plenty of comments as well as insights that will help to smoothen the rough edges of your life. These insights can even change your perception of yourself and the world around you. However, it is quite likely that you will forget today's "aha" moment once you start your activities for the following day. So, it is a good idea to make a note of all the "aha" moments. Write down what you feel and experience during the yoga session in a journal. You merely need to make a note of your observations and insights in a notebook. It might sound old school, but it is an efficient method. You can even make a list of all the poses you practice along with the new ones that you learn in each session. It will help you to keep track of all that you learn. Also, make a list of all the new terms that you learn. If you have any queries when you meditate, make it a point to list those as well. The premise is to journalize all that you feel while you do yoga. You never know, a brilliant idea might strike you, and if you don't note it down, you might forget about that idea.

Tip #2 - Be creative

As a beginner, you might find it difficult to remember all the movements that need to be done in a pose. If you face such a difficulty, you can draw the pose. Basic stick figures can help you retain the essential information about a position. Now is the time to unleash your inner artist. You can use arrows to mark the movements that go with a pose. When you do this once, the asana will be forever etched into your memory. It is not just that, but it is also a fantastic way to recollect all that you did during a yoga session. Alternatively, you can also download the pictures of the asanas from the Internet and create a yoga scrapbook for reference. Well, either of these options works well, and it is up to you. The idea is to remember the yoga postures so that you don't have to check what needs to be done while you practice yoga.

Tip #3 - You need some space

You need to allocate a designated spot to do yoga if you want to practice yoga at home. Create a place of peace to do yoga. Always select the room with the least distractions. Keep all your electronic gadgets away or in silent mode when you do yoga. You need to avoid all distractions if you want to make the most of the yoga session. The idea is to create a sacred space so that your mind and body can relax. This should be a spot where you can let go of all your worldly problems to concentrate on yourself. You can add oriental rugs and statues to give the room a calming effect. The place you select must be well ventilated with soothing lighting. You cannot practice yoga with loud music blaring on the speakers so avoid this.

Tip #4 Define your practice
The yoga routine you create depends solely on your requirements. You must explicitly define the time you can allocate towards your yoga session. Not just that, you must also decide the techniques you want to focus on. You need to strike a balance between meditation, breathing exercises and the practice of asanas. If you are not sure how to go about it, then here are a few details you can take into consideration. Do you understand the order of the yoga poses you want to include? Are there are any specific poses that you want to focus on? Do you have to learn more about any asanas you wish to incorporate? If a particular pose seems too complicated for you, is there any way in which you can simplify it? What are the asanas that you are good at? What are the different methods of relaxation and meditation that you want to include? If you have any doubts about any of these questions, please refer to the relevant chapters of this book! All the information that you need to start practicing yoga is explained within the pages of this book.

Tip #5 - A good sticky mat

A might seem silly, but a sticky mat is essential. You must never underestimate the importance of sound footing while doing yoga. In the past, if you have never used a yoga mat, you can perhaps borrow one and get a feel for it. Alternatively, you can go to a local sporting goods store and check a couple of yoga mats. The mat needs to provide excellent grip so that you can perform the yoga poses effortlessly, especially those poses where you need to stretch your limbs and torso.

Tip #6 Balance is important

Yoga is so much more than different asanas that you perform. Your yoga routine must include asanas as well as relaxation techniques. There needs to be a right balance between these two aspects of yoga if you want to attain all the benefits that yoga offers. Some might want to concentrate on the meditational aspects of yoga, while others might want to focus on the physical health benefits that it provides. Regardless of what your goal is, you need to make sure that you include breathing techniques, meditative exercises as well as asanas into your yoga routine.

Tip #7 Learn a little Sanskrit

If new languages interest you, and you want to learn a new language, then you can start with a couple of Sanskrit words. Sanskrit is an ancient language, and it includes a lot of technical words. All the yoga related vocabulary is in Sanskrit. It is a good idea to get yourself acquainted with the necessary yoga jargon. Once you are comfortable with essential pronunciation, you don't have to fumble with words. Most of the syllables in Sanskrit end with vowels and start with consonants. Also, all the letters in Sanskrit have fixed pronunciation, unlike in English. If you get a grip of the letters in Sanskrit, it is quite easy to learn Sanskrit words.

Tip #8 - Breathing breaks

You can efficiently manage the stress you experience through breathing exercises. When you concentrate on your breathing, it helps to diffuse a moment of anxiety, panic or even stress. However, you need to think about extending these breathing breaks and use them regularly in your daily life. When you use these breaks frequently, even if it lasts only a couple of minutes at a time, you will notice a positive change in your attitude. It will enable you to become better at managing stress. During your work hours, take a break for a few minutes. Whenever you take a break, close your eyes and focus all your attention on your breathing. You can perhaps count the number of breaths you take. It will assist you in overcoming any stress that you experience. It also helps to relax your respiratory muscles. Ensure that you include simple breathing exercises into your daily routine.

Tip #9 - Let the posture do its work

At times, it might feel like you need to do something while you perform an asana. It takes a little effort to master a pose. However, when you perform a pose, you need to sit back and let the pose work for you. Whenever you do a breathing exercise, you need to concentrate on your breath and nothing else. There isn't anything else that you can or must do but focus on your breathing. So, don't think that you aren't doing anything. Enjoy the exercise you perform, and you will feel better. Too much effort is as undesirable as too little effort. For instance, whenever you perform the corpse pose, merely lie down and let the posture work for you.

Tip #10 - Sleep is essential

Waking up early, doing yoga, having a good breakfast and a quick stroll around the block sounds great, doesn't it? However, it will merely be an idea if you burn yourself out. If you don't give your body the rest it deserves, you cannot perform all that you want. If you stay up late at night, it becomes nearly impossible to wake up early in the morning. Even if you manage to wake up early, the chances are that you will not feel too relaxed. You need to realize that your body is not an accurate machine and it deserves to rest. You need to sleep for at least 7 hours a night. It is okay to burn the midnight oil every once in a while. However, it is a terrible idea to turn nocturnal. Without the necessary rest, you will not feel good about yourself.

Tip #11 Ignore the critics

You will always find people who have something negative to say. Ignore all those voices in and around you that keep saying that you haven't accomplished anything. Ignore all those voices that tell yoga isn't helpful. Cynics will never say anything useful. So, it is indeed a good idea to ignore them. Practice yoga regularly and stick to your schedule. After a couple of weeks, you will undoubtedly notice a positive change in your overall health.

Chapter Eight: Yoga Plan

It's now time to create and implement your yoga practice sessions. If you want to adopt this kind of workout, first, ask yourself whether you are willing to commit to yoga practice sessions in the long run. Be honest so that you can design a plan properly. For starters, a short program will do the trick.

The final step in this book is to create a personal yoga routine. Be realistic and instead of adhering to a generalized yoga plan, make one based on your lifestyle and preference.

By coming up with your routine, you increase your chances of following through with yoga practice sessions. Given the fact that you're still at the beginning stages, you could be less prone to getting tired of the workouts if you were the one who selected each element in your plan.

Devising an Effective Yoga Plan
Devise a yoga routine that fits with your lifestyle, as well as your schedule. For instance, if you work a regular office job that requires a 9 to 5 attendance, create a plan based on this

information. If the goal is to perform a batch of yoga workouts twice a day (i.e., once in the morning and once in the evening), make sure that you have enough time to accomplish the exercises.

Important reminders:

Avoid disregarding physical conditions or any health issue. As mentioned, you need to be realistic. If unfit to perform certain poses, opt for others. This book covers 20 different yoga poses, and there are hundreds more that you're yet to discover

Avoid the modification of specific asanas. If you find them too challenging at your initial try, don't tweak them to fit your current abilities. Instead, rely on gradual improvements. For instance, if a pose involves reaching for your toes, you should reach for your toes. You may be unable to have sufficient flexibility for the meantime, but eventually, you will improve.

Choose yoga poses and yoga sequences accordingly. Only include those that you're sure will work for your personality type. For instance, if you're the type who can get easily bored when lying down on your back, consider staying away from too many workouts that involve lying down.

Chapter Nine: How to Practice Yoga Daily

It might not seem natural to include yoga into your daily routine. However, it does help to think about the different benefits just ten minutes of yoga offers. You can enhance your overall physical and mental health with yoga. If you can only set some time aside for yoga, it will be easy.

There are just two steps you have to follow to practice yoga daily. The first step is to incorporate yoga into your daily schedule. The second step is to vary your daily practice.

Step 1: Incorporate Yoga into Your Daily Schedule

Your yoga gear must be handy. If you want to practice yoga daily, then make sure that your yoga gear is always laid out. If you do this, then you won't be able to find any excuses not to do yoga daily. You need a yoga mat, maybe a yoga belt, blanket and even a block. However, a simple yoga mat is sufficient for a beginner. You can buy the necessary yoga props from any sporting goods stores or also order them online. You don't need any specific yoga clothing per se. As long as your clothes are comfortable and don't constrain your movements, you are good to go. Anything that you can wear to the gym is suitable for yoga as well. Once you have all the necessary yoga gear, the next step is to decide when to practice and how long you want to practice.

There is no such thing as the perfect time to do yoga. However, if you want to include yoga into your daily schedule, then it is a good idea to practice it at the same time daily. It will help you to create a routine. You can practice it early in the morning if you are an early riser. Doing yoga first thing in the morning will leave you feeling energized. Also, it will prevent you from making any excuses to skip yoga later in the day. You can practice it in the evening if you want to. It is better to create a routine. Once you fix a specific time to do yoga, it does get easy. Your body and mind will associate a particular time and place with your yoga session. Select a time slot when there won't be any distractions or the distractions will be minimal, like early in the morning or late at night. You can practice yoga for as long as you want. It can be a couple of sets of Surya Namaskars (sun salutations) or even 90 minutes and a full session.

Set a specific time for yoga. Make sure that you turn off all your electronic gadgets or at least put them on silent. Create a calm space for yourself without any distractions. Most of the yoga classes last for 60 to 95 minutes. You don't have to practice yoga in one go; you can even practice it in sets of ten minutes if you want to. The spot that you choose for yoga needs to be comfortable. It must be peaceful and have soft lighting. It must not be too cold or hot. You can even join a yoga class if you want to. If you have access to a garden, you can practice yoga in the garden. Regardless of where you want to practice yoga, the place must have room for plenty of movement.

You will experience a gradual change in your overall health when you practice yoga daily. The difference won't be overnight, and it does take a while. At times, you might even feel like you aren't progressing. Give it some time and be consistent in your efforts. You certainly will see a change. If you do miss one session of yoga, don't make a big deal of it. It is okay and you can continue from where you left off previously.

Step Two: Vary Your Daily Practice
The key is to be regular, not rigorous. It is better to practice yoga daily for a couple of minutes instead of a lengthy session on an irregular basis. Start with any asana you want to do, but don't start with really complicated ones. Regardless of

the pose that you want to begin with, perfect it before you move on to something else. It is okay to do some yoga instead of none and do remind yourself of this. Have a positive and not a negative mindset towards yoga. Don't worry if you don't get a pose correct. Try again. Don't tell yourself that you cannot do something. You certainly can do any pose if you practice a little. Practice yoga regularly and you can slowly move on to the more difficult ones.

The next step is to create a sequence of yoga poses to practice. It can be a challenging step, mainly if you practice yoga at home. Set up a different series that you can practice daily. The key is to get all the benefits of yoga without getting bored. If you practice the same sequence daily, you will end up getting bored. You can start the practice with meditation and some chanting exercises to clear your mind. It will also help you to focus your thoughts. Before you begin to practice, think about the reasons that motivate you. If you cannot think of a specific purpose, go through the list of advantages yoga offers. Then you can move onto to warm up exercises like the Surya Namaskars. Always end your yoga session with something that relaxes you. Design your yoga schedule in such a manner that it contains easy and challenging poses.

It is entirely reasonable that you won't be able to do all the yoga asanas every day. You can incorporate poses from all the types of asanas into your daily schedule so that it doesn't bore you. Start with the asanas that are easy, and you can slowly move onto the poses that are more difficult. Perform poses from each of the asanas in this order: Standing poses, inversions, then the backbends and lastly the forward bends. To elevate the stress on your spine between the backbends and the forward bends, add a twisting asana. You must be able to hold each of the asanas for at least 3 to 5 breaths. Always end your yoga session with the corpse pose. It will relax your body and calm your mind as well.

If you like to chant mantras before or after your yoga session, then do so. However, make sure that you change the chant daily. There are different mantras that you can use, and each of these mantras tends to correspond with your intention. The repetition of a mantra will distract you from the stress you feel, and it will also help you to maintain your focus. The most basic mantra is Om or Aum. It is quite powerful and chanting this mantra and it will fill your body with positive vibrations. It is usually combined with the "Shanti" mantra. Shanti in Sanskrit means peace. You can repeat Om as many times as you want to. There is another mantra that's known as the maha-mantra. The maha or the great mantra is to chant "Hare Krishna." It usually helps to bring you mental peace. You have to keep repeating the words "Hare Krishna" over and over again. Another mantra that you can chant is "Lokah Samantha Sukhino Bhavantu." This mantra helps to foster happiness and freedom. Repeat this mantra three times or even more than that if you want to. The mantras that you chant in yoga have one purpose, to calm your mind and bring you peace. It is quite easy to incorporate yoga into your daily schedule. All that matters is whether you want to do it daily or not.

Chapter Ten: FAQ's For Yoga Beginner's

Since you are a yoga beginner, it is quite likely that you will have certain queries and doubts. Yoga might seem like an intimidating practice to start with, but you don't have to worry. You will undoubtedly find yoga enjoyable and relaxing. The information in this chapter will help you to get started quickly.

What style of yoga should I practice?

There are different styles of yoga these days. You need to select a method that meets your requirements. There are certain things you must take into consideration while you choose a yoga style. The factors you need to consider are your age, the level of activity you are comfortable with and your fitness goals. Some forms of yoga are fast-paced while others are slow. Some types of yoga include a lot of meditation while some concentrate on breathing techniques. You can quickly experiment with different combinations of yoga until you find something that you enjoy. Make sure that your yoga routine includes Asanas, breathing techniques, as well as some meditation. A perfect balance of these three aspects will help to improve your overall wellbeing. According to your goals, you can emphasize on each of these aspects. For instance, if weight-loss is your primary goal, then you should include a lot of yoga Asanas like Surya Namaskars.

Do I need a yoga teacher?

Not necessarily. You don't need a yoga teacher. If you are good at following instructions, then this book is the only yoga teacher you will need. The instructions in this book are easy to understand and follow. If you are not able to understand any of the yoga poses discussed in this book, open YouTube and search for the pose you need. Yoga is not rocket science. Follow the instructions, listen to your body and you are good to go.

Can I eat before doing yoga?

It is advisable that you don't eat anything immediately before doing yoga. Yoga is a form of exercise, and as with any other type of activity, it is ideal to exercise on an empty stomach. However, if you find that you are low on energy, you can always have a small snack before the yoga session. It is a good idea to give your body at least an hour's break after the meal before you do yoga. The best time to do yoga is early in the morning. It will help to give your day an energetic boost. It will calm your mind and refresh your body.

What about flexibility? You don't have to be flexible to practice yoga. Yoga helps to increase your flexibility. After a couple of weeks of yoga, your body will feel more limber and flexible. So, you don't have to worry about your flexibility initially. It is okay if you cannot touch your toes when you bend forwards. After a couple of days, you will be able to reach your toes effortlessly.

Is yoga safe if I am overweight?
Your weight, fitness level, and size doesn't matter. Anyone can practice yoga. In fact, yoga is an ideal form of exercise to lose weight. The yoga asanas couple with different breathing and meditative techniques will help to detoxify your body and cleanse your system. Yoga helps to decrease stress, which is a primary reason for obesity these days. When you tackle the underlying factors that are the reason for weight gain, it leads to weight loss. If you want to build lean muscle without bulking up, then yoga is the best form of exercise. It helps to tone your body, improve your core strength, and strengthen your muscles.

Is yoga a religious practice?

Yoga is not a religious practice, and it will not cause any conflict with any religions. Yoga is a merely a form of exercise and nothing more than that. It is a combination of physical Asanas, breathing exercises, and meditative techniques that release stress. Yoga also helps you to come in touch with your spiritual side. Since the ancient times, yoga is used as a means to connect with the cosmos. When you are calm and relaxed, you can easily connect with your spiritual side.

Do I need to have black pants to do yoga?

Whenever someone says yoga, the first thing that probably comes to your mind is people in stretchy yoga pants. Black yoga pants are quite popular these days. However, there is no strict dress code that you need to follow to perform yoga. Wear clothes that make you feel comfortable. The clothes you opt for must allow you to move freely. As long as the clothes don't restrict your movements, you are good to go.

How frequently do I need to do yoga?

It is a good idea to practice yoga daily. Even if your yoga session doesn't exceed 15 minutes, try to practice yoga daily. The best time to practice yoga is as soon as you wake up in the morning. If you think that you will not be able to do yoga daily, then make it a point to do yoga at least thrice a week. You don't have to go to a yoga class to do yoga! You can practice yoga in your living room itself!

Is yoga time-consuming?

Yoga is not a time-consuming practice. A session of yoga can last anywhere between 15 minutes to an hour. It depends on your schedule and your level of fitness. However, if you take into consideration the different benefits it offers, yoga will not feel like a time-consuming exercise. Plan your week in such a manner that you can allocate a couple of minutes to do yoga daily.

Is yoga a strenuous exercise?

Unlike HIIT or any other form of intensive cardio, yoga is not a strenuous exercise. Even if you are out of shape, yoga will not feel like a stressful exercise to you. As a beginner, you must always start with the basic yoga poses and work your way toward the advanced poses. However, make sure that you include at least a couple of Surya Namaskars into your yoga routine. In the initial stages, engage in meditative exercises and breathing techniques.

Conclusion

Thank you again for choosing this book!

I hope this book helped you to learn the basics of yoga. By now, you are well aware of the different mental, physical and spiritual benefits that yoga offers. Yoga is an excellent form of exercise to improve your overall wellbeing. Now that you know about the different yoga poses, breathing exercises and meditation techniques, all that you need to do is get started as soon as possible.

Make use of the various tips in this book to create a yoga routine that suits your needs. The FAQs answered in this book will clear up all the doubts you have about yoga. Yoga is an easy form of exercise to perform. If you piously stick to your yoga routine for at least two weeks, you will see a positive change in your physical and mental health! So, all that is left for you to do is to get started.

Thank you and all the best!

Susan Mori

Sources

https://www.care2.com/greenliving/12-yoga-tips-for-beginners.html

http://www.onepowerfulword.com/2010/10/18-benefits-of-deep-breathing-and-how.html

https://www.artofliving.org/in-en/yoga/yoga-benefits

https://blog.mindvalley.com/15-faqs-for-yoga-beginners/

https://www.verywellfit.com/essential-beginner-yoga-tips-3566732

Other Book By Susan Mori

Printed in Great Britain
by Amazon

16582613R00061